LOOKING BACK

THE WORLD OF ISLAM

00

ARTELL

Evans Brothers Limited
2A Portman Mansions
Chiltern Street
London W1M 1LE

First published 1998

British Library Cataloguing in Publication Data

Martell, Hazel Mary
The world of Islam : before 1700. - (Looking back)
1.Islam - History - Juvenile literature
I.Title
297'.09

ISBN 0237517264

Editor: Nicola Barber
Designer: Neil Sayer
Picture research: Victoria Brooker
Maps: Nick Hawken
Production: Jenny Mulvanny

Consultant: Shahrukh Husain

Printed in Spain by GRAFO, S.A. - Bilbao

Acknowledgements

Cover (main image) Trip/A Tovy (background image) Bibliotheque Nationale, Paris/Bridgeman Art Library **Title page** Werner Forman Archive **page 7** Christine Osborne Pictures **page 8** Robert Harding Picture Library **page 9** Werner Forman Archive **page 10** Peter Sanders Photography **page 11** Peter Sanders Photography **page 12** Bibliotheque Nationale, Paris/Bridgeman Art Library **page 13** Werner Forman Archive **page 15** David Lomax/Robert Harding Picture Library **page 17** Peter Sanders Photography **page 19** Trip/Trip **page 20** Peter Sanders Photography **page 21** Ancient Art and Architecture **page 22** Werner Forman Archive **page 23** Getty Images **page 24** (top) Ancient Art and Architecture (bottom) Trip/Trip **page 25** Trip/Trip **page 26** Peter Sanders Photography **page 27** (top) Peter Sanders Photography (bottom) Trip/Trip **page 29** Trip/Trip **page 30** Peter Sanders Photography **page 32** Werner Forman Archive **page 33** Christine Osborne Pictures **page 34** Bibliotheque Nationale, Paris/Bridgeman Art Library **page 35** Robert Harding Picture Library **page 37** Getty Images **page 38** Peter Sanders Photography **page 39** Robert Harding Picture Library **page 40** Ancient Art and Architecture **page 42** Ancient Art and Architecture **page 43** Trip/V Kolpakov **page 44** Ancient Art and Architecture **page 45** Robert Harding Picture Library **page 46** Werner Forman Archive **page 47** (top) Werner Forman Archive (bottom) Ancient Art and Architecture **page 48** Ancient Art and Architecture **page 49** Louvre, Paris/Bridgeman Art Library **page 50** Trip/TH-Foto Werbung **page 51** Trip/Trip **page 52** (top) Peter Sanders Photography (bottom) Getty Images **page 53** Ancient Art and Architecture **page 55** (top and bottom) Ancient Art and Architecture **page 57** Ancient Art and Architecture **page 58** Robert Harding Picture Library **page 59** Trip/H Rogers

CONTENTS

CHAPTER ONE

INTRODUCTION

Islam is the name of the religion practised by Muslims. It means 'submission to the will of Allah', which is the Muslim name for God, and it is now one of the major religions of the world. It is based on the teachings of the Prophet Muhammad, who was born in Makka in Arabia around the year 570 CE.

A CLOSER LOOK

CE stands for 'in the Common Era'. It is often used in dates instead of AD. In the same way, BCE 'Before the Common Era' is used instead of BC. However, the system for counting years is the same whichever abbreviation is used.

Islam is the fastest-growing religion in the world today, but in this book we look at how and why it expanded from the time of Muhammad to the end of the 16th century, when three powerful Islamic empires controlled much of India and the Middle East. We examine the effect Islam had on its followers' everyday lives, their arts and crafts, and their science and technology in the first 1000 years after Muhammad's birth.

ARABIA BEFORE MUHAMMAD

In the 6th century CE, Arabia was the name given to the whole of the peninsula of land between the Red Sea in the west and the Persian (or Arabian) Gulf in

A CLOSER LOOK

Arabic is the language of Islam. Its alphabet has 28 letters, but they look very different from the Roman alphabet used in most European languages. Because of this, the names of people and places from the world of Islam often have two or three different spellings when they are translated into another language. For example, Muhammad's name is sometimes written as Mohammed or Mohamet, and the *Quran* is sometimes written as the *Koran*. The Hijra is sometimes the Hajira, while Makka is also Mecca and Makkah, and Madina is also Medina and Madinah.

the east. Its total area was around 2,590,000 square kilometres, but in spite of its size, the population of Arabia was small. This was because most of the land was hot desert, with an annual rainfall of less than 100 millimetres and summer temperatures that could reach over 50° Centigrade. This made agriculture impossible, except around the scattered oases, along the coastal plain to the west and in the highlands to the south where there was a higher rainfall.

Some settlements developed around the oases, but most people led nomadic lives, following their herds of sheep, goats or camels from one place to another in search of water and grazing. Others made a living through trade, either by buying and selling goods themselves or by offering services to the many camel trains that crossed the country from east to west and from north to south. These services included the provision of food, drink and shelter for the traders and their pack animals, and also protection from attacks by robbers and bandits.

An oasis in the United Arab Emirates. Oases are some of the few places in Arabia where trees can grow.

A CLOSER LOOK
Although the nomadic tribes often fought against each other, they were famous for their hospitality, especially towards travellers in the desert. A stranger could go to any nomad's tent and know that he or she would be given food, drink and hospitality for up to three days before travelling on. This was because everyone recognised that the desert was a dangerous and unpredictable place in which any traveller could easily get into difficulties and die.

MANY DIFFERENT TRIBES

The people of Arabia were divided into many different tribes, each of which was then divided into clans. Every clan had its own chief, or shaikh. Some clans led a settled life, while others were nomads. In spite of this, there were strong ties within each tribe, and families who belonged to settled clans often sent their young sons to live with nomadic relations and learn the ways of the desert for a few years.

All the tribes had a similar way of life, spoke the same language and lived by the same unwritten rules, but they were often at war with each other and took great delight in raiding each other's camel herds or even kidnapping members of another tribe. Occasionally the members of two or more tribes would join together to fight a common enemy. Then, in the 7th century, the Islamic religion united them in a way that nothing had ever done before, inspiring them to go out and conquer large parts of the world.

Buildings such as the Sultan Han, a 13th-century caravanserai *near Konya in Turkey, help us to understand more about life in the Islamic world.*

HOW DO WE KNOW?

We know about the first 1000 years of the world of Islam from many different sources. The most important are the *Quran*, which is the Muslims' Holy Book, and the *Hadith*, which are collections of Muhammad's thoughts and advice on everyday life and its problems. These two sources tell us much about Islamic beliefs and the laws which govern a Muslim's life. Other written sources, besides general historical works, include accounts of journeys undertaken by Muslims and collections of stories.

This tile from the Ottoman Empire shows a plan of the Kaaba (see page 11) and the surrounding buildings in Makka. The writing above the plan is from the Quran *and instructs all Muslims to go on a pilgrimage to Makka, if they are able to.*

Many buildings from the period are still standing. There are numerous mosques, as well as tombs and shrines, palaces, castles and houses. Along the trade routes the remains of *caravanserais* can be found. There are also many artefacts from the period, including glass and pottery, paintings, metalwork and textiles, all of which help us to build up a picture of what life was like in the Islamic world.

CHAPTER TWO

MAKKA - BIRTHPLACE OF MUHAMMAD

Modern Makka is a city of over 550,000 people. At its centre is the Kaaba. In this picture you can see the top of one of the six minarets of the Sacred Enclosure, which surrounds the Kaaba.

Makka was a wealthy city and a centre of pilgrimage long before the prophet Muhammad was born there in around 570 CE. Although it was surrounded by mountains and deserts, it received enough rainfall over the winter months to keep its wells filled with water and so people could live there all year round.

THE FOUNDATION OF MAKKA

Makka stands in the Valley of Ibrahim at a point where it is joined by passes through the mountains from the north, south and west. The valley is named after the prophet Ibrahim, who is known in the Jewish and Christian religions as Abraham. Although he lived many centuries before Muhammad was born, the *Quran* tells us that Ibrahim also believed that there was one God, called Allah. One day, Allah decided to test Ibrahim's faith and so he told him to take his slave-wife Hagar and their baby son Ismail into the desert and leave them there to fend for themselves. Ibrahim loved Hagar and his son, but he knew he had to obey Allah's will and so he left them in a place between the hills of Al-Safa and Al-Marwa. As Ismail grew thirsty and sick from the heat, Hagar ran back and forth between the two hills, desperately searching for water and praying

A CLOSER LOOK
After Hagar died, both Ibrahim and Ismail settled in Makka, where Ismail married a woman from the tribe of Jurhum. They had 12 sons who were said to be the founders of the twelve tribes of Arabia.

for a miracle. Suddenly a spring of clear water bubbled up at Ismail's feet and his life was saved. The stream became known as Zamzam. As it kept flowing, people were attracted to come and settle near it and the town of Makka gradually grew up around it.

THE BUILDING OF THE KAABA

In the centre of Makka there is a building known as the Kaaba. It is now the holiest shrine of Islam, but nobody knows its exact history as it was already very old when Muhammad was born. There are at least two accounts of when and why it was built. One says that it was first built by Adam to represent the Kingdom of Heaven on Earth and then later rebuilt by Ibrahim, with the help of Ismail, to thank Allah for saving Ismail's life. The other says that Ibrahim and Ismail built it from new. Both accounts agree that it was originally built for the worship of the One God, Allah.

A CLOSER LOOK
In the western wall of the Kaaba there is a large stone, known as the Black Stone. Legend says that when Adam found it in the desert it gleamed white and shone in the sunlight, but the wickedness of the people on Earth eventually turned it black. Another legend says that the angels took the Black Stone to heaven for safe-keeping at the time of the Great Flood and later returned it to Ibrahim when he and Ismail were rebuilding the Kaaba.

Pilgrims visiting the Kaaba today

Chapter Two

Gods of the desert

Ismail lived near the Kaaba for the rest of his life, but his descendants were ousted from Makka by another desert tribe called the Amalekites. Unlike Ibrahim and Ismail, the Amalekites believed in many different gods and goddesses and used the Kaaba as a place to worship them. These goddesses included Manat who was the goddess of fortune and Al-Lat, the goddess of the sun. There were gods of trees and springs, as well as gods of large stones and rocky outcrops. Some people also believed that there was one supreme God who ruled over all the others. Statues of the gods were placed inside the Kaaba and soon people from all over Arabia started making pilgrimages to Makka once or twice each year.

Two travellers pass a typical Arabian village. In the background one goat is drinking water from a pond and another is grazing. On the right, someone is spinning yarn by hand, ready for weaving into cloth.

The wealth of Makka

As well as attracting pilgrims, Makka was in a good position for merchants and traders from Arabia and further afield, as trade routes linking Africa to Asia and the Far East to the Mediterranean passed through the town. The Makkans took advantage of this by providing services for foreign traders, and by charging the foreigners import and export taxes on all goods passing in and out of the city, plus a tax on each caravan train and another tax on any goods sold locally. The twice-yearly pilgrimage seasons also generated a great deal of wealth. Not only did

A present-day camel train crossing the desert in the United Arab Emirates. In the past, as well as being beasts of burden, camels provided meat and milk for the Bedouin. Their hair was spun into yarn and their skin was made into leather.

visiting pilgrims keep the local hostelries busy, they also spent large amounts of money in Makka's many markets and shops.

A NEW WAY OF LIFE

As Makka grew in size and wealth, more and more people left the nomadic life of the desert and settled down in the city, often becoming merchants or traders, or providing services for pilgrims and their families. Many of them became rich and were able to live in luxury. Many of the people of Makka forgot the old ways of the desert. They no longer offered free hospitality to those in need. The poor and the sick were left to fend for themselves, while women and children, servants and slaves were often treated with cruelty and violence.

A CLOSER LOOK

Although the wells around Makka provided water for the people in the city and their animals, there was not enough water to grow crops such as corn or wheat. All grain products had to be brought by camel trains from countries to the north, such as Syria and Jordan. Early Arab traders exchanged leather goods, spices, frankincense and myrrh for grain, but later they traded for goods from all around the world, including silk, pottery and porcelain from China, jewels from India, furs from the Viking lands and gold, ivory and slaves from Africa.

Chapter Three

The Life of Muhammad

Muslims believe that Muhammad was the last and most important prophet of Allah. They have great respect for him and usually add the words "Peace be unto him" after his name each time they say it. There was nothing in his early life, however, to suggest that he would become a great religious leader and affect the lives of millions of people all across the world with his teachings.

Muhammad's childhood

Muhammad was born in Makka in about 570 on the 12th day of the third month of the Muslim calendar. His mother, Amina, was of the Hashemite clan which was part of the tribe of Quraish. His father, Abdullah, was also of the tribe of Quraish and was the son of Abdul Muttalib who was the head of the council of elders in Makka at that time. The Quraish was one of the most important tribes in Arabia as it was responsible for looking after the Kaaba (see page 11). The Kaaba was to become the most sacred site in the world of Islam, but at the time of Muhammad's birth it still contained statues and images of many different gods of the desert.

A closer look

The Muslim year is slightly shorter than the year used in the Christian world. It still contains 12 months, but each one starts when a new moon is seen. The new year starts after 12 months have passed. This means that New Year is not on the same day every year. It also means that important events are celebrated at different times each year. For example, the month of Ramadan can fall in spring, summer, autumn or winter. The names of the months are (1) Muharram, (2) Safar, (3) Rabi-ul-Awwal, (4) Rabi-ul-Akhir, (5) Jumada al-Ula, (6) Jumada al-Akhira, (7) Rajab, (8) Sha'ban, (9) Ramadan, (10) Shawwal, (11) Dhul-Qa'da, and (12) Dhul-Hijja.

Bedouin men and boys gather to drink tea and coffee in Saudi Arabia today. Although the stove is modern, the tea will be sweet and served without milk, and the coffee will be strong and flavoured with cardomom, just as they were when Muhammad was a young boy.

In spite of his important relations, Muhammad's early years were spent in poverty, for his father died before he was born and his mother was in poor health. Amina followed Arab traditions and sent Muhammad to be brought up in the desert around Makka in the family of a Bedouin woman, called Halima. In the desert Muhammad learned about the importance of hospitality towards strangers and about helping the poor and the sick, widows and orphans. He became experienced at surviving in harsh conditions, sometimes with very little food or water. He probably also learned how to ride a horse and use a sword. In quiet moments he listened to the poems of love, war and history for which the Bedouin were famous.

When Muhammad was six years old, Amina died. For the next two years his grandfather, Abdul Muttalib, looked after him. Then Abdul Muttalib died too and Muhammad's uncle, Abu Talib, took over care of the eight-year-old boy.

Chapter Three

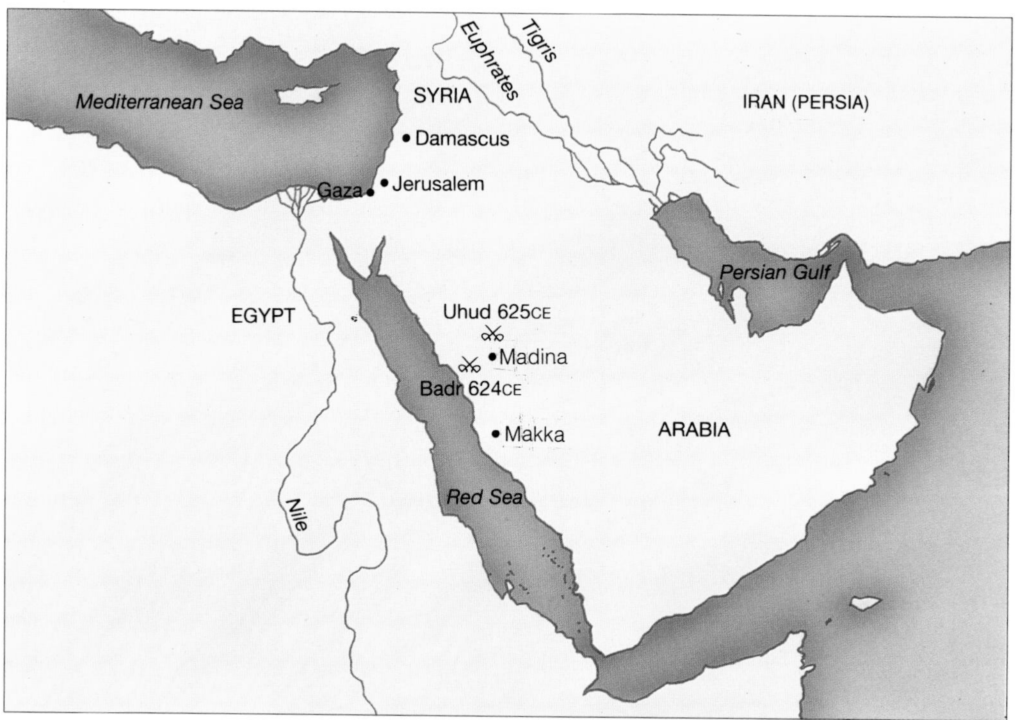

This map shows the most important places connected with Muhammad's life.

Muhammad as a young man

Once he was old enough, Muhammad helped to look after flocks of sheep belonging to his nomadic relatives. From the age of 12, he started going with Abu Talib on trading journeys north to Syria. Muhammad and his uncle probably visited the cities of Damascus and Gaza, both of which had busy markets where they traded for grain and other goods.

Muhammad worked for his uncle until he was about 25 years old and in this time he became well-known for his honesty and his wisdom. People called him Al-Amin, which means 'The Trustworthy' or 'The Truthful', and valued his opinion on many different problems. For example, at one time the Kaaba needed some repairs and the Black Stone had to be moved until the work was completed. When the time came for the Black Stone to be replaced, members of the various tribes in Makka started to quarrel over which of them should carry it.

A closer look

There are no paintings or carvings to show us exactly what Muhammad looked like, but we know from descriptions that he was fairly tall and well-built. He was also strong and very energetic. His hair and his beard were dark and a little curly and his eyes were light brown. He was fond of children and kind to animals, and often spoke up in their defence.

Muhammad solved the problem by spreading a blanket on the ground and lifting the Black Stone on to it. He then told the heads of the tribes each to take hold of a corner of the blanket and lift it up, so that they could all carry the Black Stone together.

MARRIAGE TO KHADIJA

Muhammad's reputation for honesty eventually brought him to the attention of Khadija, the widow of a wealthy merchant in Makka. She offered him a job looking after the camel train on which she was sending goods to Syria. Muhammad accepted her offer and in due course returned from Syria with a good profit. This impressed Khadija still further and, although she was a few years older than Muhammad, she suggested that they got married. Muhammad agreed and they went on to have several children, but only one daughter, Fatima, lived long enough to marry and have children of her own.

Muslims still visit the cave at Hira, where Muhammad had his first visions.

THE CAVE AT HIRA

Although Muhammad was happily married and ran a successful business with Khadija, there were times when he wanted to be by himself. He was a thoughtful man and liked to go into the desert to meditate on life and on what was happening in the world around him. His favourite place was a cave at Hira in the mountains near Makka. When he was about 40 years old, Muhammad had the first of many visions in which an angel came to him in the cave with a message from God, or Allah. Muhammad could neither read nor write and so he had to learn the messages by heart. Later he told them to his followers and eventually they were written down in the *Quran*, which is the Holy Book of Islam. The most important of these messages was that there was just one God, whose name was Allah.

For three years Muhammad told only his family and a few close friends about his visions. Then Allah sent him a message to start preaching to the people of Makka, in order to persuade them to give up their old gods and worship Allah instead.

A CLOSER LOOK
When he preached to the people of Makka, Muhammad said that they should, "Visit the sick, feed the hungry and free the captives." He also told them that, "Wealth comes from a contented heart, not from a lot of possessions." This was just the opposite of what many of the rich and powerful Makkans believed and it made them very angry.

The Hijra

The first people to accept Muhammad's teachings were his wife, Khadija, his servant, Zaid, and his ten-year-old cousin, Ali. When he started preaching to the people of Makka, many of the poor people, the slaves and the labourers listened to his message. But very few of the wealthy people wanted to believe him. They did not like being told that they were wicked sinners. They also thought that if people no longer worshipped the idols in the Kaaba then the twice-yearly pilgrimages would stop and Makka would lose a lot of money. So they said that Muhammad was mad or telling lies. They persecuted many of his followers, locking them up and insulting them, beating and torturing them. Some were even killed for their beliefs.

Muhammad was concerned by the way his followers were treated, and he knew that his own life was in danger, too. Then, in 619 CE, Khadija died, followed closely by Muhammad's uncle, Abu Talib. This added to the danger Muhammad was in because Abu Talib had supported and protected Muhammad and his followers as much as possible.

By this time Muhammad's fame as a preacher had spread beyond Makka, and in 622 CE a group of men from Yathrib invited him to go and preach to them. Their city was in a large oasis about 320 kilometres to the north of Makka. Muhammad accepted the

A CLOSER LOOK
The date of the Hijra, 622 CE, was chosen as the start of the Muslim calendar. Muslims put the letters AH after dates later than this to show that they are 'After the Hijra'.

invitation and, with his friend Abu-Bakr, he left Makka and set out for Yathrib. This journey is known as the Hijra.

MUHAMMAD IN YATHRIB

Muhammad was made welcome in Yathrib and soon settled down and built himself a house. He and Abu-Bakr sent for their families to come and join them and Muhammad married Abu-Bakr's daughter, Ayesha. Many people came to listen to his message and soon started following the new religion. It became so popular that Yathrib became known as Madinat-ul-Rasul, meaning 'The City of the Prophet', or Madina Al-Munawwara, meaning 'The Enlightened City'. Later, both names were shortened to Madina and this name was used instead of Yathrib.

The people of Makka were not happy about the growing strength of the new religion, and they did all they could to cause trouble for Muhammad and his followers. There were many small fights between the two sides, as well as two important battles. The

These views of Makka and Madina are from an ancient, hand-painted book. The Mosque of the Prophet is on the left (see pages 20-1) and the Kaaba and the Sacred Enclosure are on the right.

A closer look
At the Battle of Badr there were 313 Muslims fighting against 1000 well-equipped soldiers from Makka. The Muslims had very little armour to protect themselves from injury and few horses, but they believed that their religion helped them to victory.

first was at Badr in 624 CE and was a victory for the Muslims. The two sides met again the next year at Uhud, and this battle ended in a stalemate.

The return to Makka

Although Muhammad had his closest friends and family around him in Madina, he sometimes wanted to return to Makka. But he knew that many people there remained hostile to him and would kill him if they had the chance. Then, in 628 CE, Allah told him that he would soon go back to Makka in triumph. Muhammad decided to return that year with a group of his followers. The Makkans made a treaty with him, allowing Muslims to visit their city, and Muhammad went back to Madina. However, the Makkans broke this treaty in 630 CE, so Muhammad gathered a large army together and marched to Makka. Seeing the size of the army, the Makkans surrendered without a fight and Muhammad

The Mosque of the Prophet in Madina today. It is built on the site of Muhammad's tomb and is the second most sacred place in Islam after Makka.

claimed the city for the Muslims. He threw the idols out of the Kaaba and converted the people of Makka to Islam.

After this, Muhammad went back to Madina once more and spent the next two years preaching and converting more people to Islam. But, exhausted by all his hard work, he fell ill with a fever and died on the 12th day of the month of Rabi-ul-Awwal in 11 AH. (This is the same date as 7 June 632 CE.) He was buried at the home of his wife, Ayesha, and later a mosque was built over his tomb.

A CLOSER LOOK

The *Quran* tells of Muhammad's Night Journey on which he was taken from Makka to Jerusalem, from where he ascended to Heaven and into the presence of Allah, before being returned to Makka by the following morning. Because of this, Jerusalem became the third most sacred site in the Islamic world after Makka and Madina.

This picture shows Muhammad accompanied by angels on the Night Journey to Heaven. No one is permitted to paint Muhammad's face, so it is hidden by a veil.

CHAPTER FOUR

ISLAMIC BELIEFS

A CLOSER LOOK

Although they have many differences, the religions of Islam, Judaism and Christianity also have many beliefs in common. All three religions have prophets and angels who spread the word of God. They also all have the story of the creation of the world in six days, and of Noah and the Great Flood.

The words of the Shahada are painted on this 17th-century tile from a mosque in Turkey. It also has the blessing, "God's mercy be upon him", after Muhammad's name.

Islam began with the teachings of the prophet Muhammad, but Muslims believe that it is the religion that Allah had wanted his people to follow from the beginning of time. They believe that there were other prophets before Muhammad who had tried to teach people about Allah, but for various reasons they were not successful and many of them were killed. These prophets include Ibrahim (Abraham) and Musa (Moses), who were also important to Jews and Christians. They also included 'Isa (Jesus), but Muslims believe that he, like Muhammad, was totally a human being and not the son of God.

THE FIVE PILLARS OF ISLAM

Muhammad taught his followers a new way of life, based on a system of beliefs and actions, known as the Five Pillars of Islam. These are as important to Muslims today as they were when Muhammad was alive.

The first and most important of the Five Pillars is the Shahada. This is the declaration of a person's faith that, "There is no god but Allah, and Muhammad is the messenger of Allah." These are the words used to call Muslims to prayer and the first words spoken by a person wishing to become a Muslim. They are also the first words said to a newborn baby and, if possible, the last words said to someone before he or she dies.

The second pillar is prayer itself. This is known as salat and is a set of prayers which must be said five times a day at fixed times by every Muslim over ten years old. They can be said by a person alone, or with others gathered in a mosque, but they must always be said facing in the direction of Makka. The person praying must also be wearing clean clothes if possible and must follow a ritual known as 'wudu', in which the hands, mouth, face, arms and feet are washed in pure water before prayers begin. He or she must also stand on clean ground or on a special prayer mat.

Muslims at prayer in the Sultan Abdul Aziz mosque in Kuala Lumpur, Malaysia. Prayers must be said at dawn, at noon, in the late afternoon, at dusk and after dark.

The third pillar of Islam is known as zakat and involves giving up a set proportion of one's wealth each year to help those in need, and to help build and repair mosques and colleges for Muslim students. Zakat has its origins in the hospitality shown to travellers by the nomadic tribes of the desert, and in their care of the poor, the sick and the elderly.

The fourth pillar is saum, which is the fast that takes place from sunrise to sunset every day throughout the month of Ramadan. This is to remind Muslims of the month in which Muhammad first began to receive messages from Allah and to make them think of the sufferings of the poor and the hungry. As well as fasting at this time, Muslims should also say more prayers and try to read the whole of the *Quran*.

Chapter Four

This certificate from 1432 shows the Sacred Enclosure around the Kaaba and was given as proof that the holder had been on the Hajj that year.

The final pillar is Hajj, which is the pilgrimage to Makka in the 12th month of the Islamic year, and which all healthy Muslims should try to make at least once in a lifetime. Today's pilgrims are able to fly to Saudi Arabia from all parts of the world, but in the past they had to travel overland and the journey could take many weeks, months or even years. Once they reached Makka, these pilgrims stayed in one of the many hotels or camped out in tents around the city on the Plain of Arafat, just like they do today. From there they tried to visit all the sites associated with Muhammad and the founding of their religion.

The most important site is still the Kaaba in Makka itself. Every pilgrim has to go around it seven times and touch or kiss the Black Stone in the southeast corner of the building. The pilgrims then go to pray at the Maqam Ibrahim, which was the boulder on which Ibrahim stood when he rebuilt the Kaaba. From there they drink water from the ancient well of Zamzam, before visiting the hills of Al-Safa amd Al-Marwa to remember Hagar's desperate search for water for her baby son, Ismail. After that they travel on foot or by camel to Mount Arafat from where Muhammad preached

The rock on which Ibrahim stood to build the Kaaba (see page 11) has now been placed on a marble stand inside this crystal case.

on his last pilgrimage to Makka. From Mount Arafat they travel to another hilly area, called Muzdalifa. There pilgrims can spend the night praying in the open air of the desert, before going on to the small town of Mina where they complete the Hajj by throwing stones at three carved pillars which represent the Devil. This shows that they are rejecting him, just as Muhammad had done.

Whether they have taken part in the pilgrimage that year or not, all Muslims celebrate the end of the Hajj with the festival of Eid-ul-Adha. After praying in the mosque, it is the custom for every family that can afford it to sacrifice a sheep or a lamb, eating two-thirds of it themselves and then giving the rest to the poor.

A CLOSER LOOK

At Mount Arafat the pilgrims listen to a special sermon, preached from one of a flight of steps which run up the mountainside. This is the step where Muhammad stood to give a sermon on his last pilgrimage.

Modern pilgrims camping on the Plain of Arafat. Mount Arafat is in the background.

Chapter Four

The *Quran*

Muslims believe that the *Quran* contains the actual words of Allah, as told to Muhammad by the Angel Jibril (Gabriel). They also believe that this same message was passed on to other prophets, such as Moses and Jesus, but that other people then changed it for their own purposes. To prevent this happening to the message in the *Quran*, its words have not been altered since they were first delivered.

The message within the *Quran* is divided into 114 chapters, or suras, each of which is made up

A closer look

Muslims treat any copy of the *Quran* with great respect. To prevent it getting dirty or damaged whilst being read, it is often placed on a special stand which is usually made from wood. Many of these are plain, but some, especially those that are used in mosques, are elaborately carved.

A Muslim man reads the Quran *inside the Mosque of the Prophet in Madina. The holy book is placed on a special stand so that it does not get bent, torn or dirtied.*

of a number of verses. The *Quran* is arranged according to the length of the suras, the longest at the beginning and the shortest at the end. The early suras revealed to Muhammad are about Allah, about Muhammad's role as his prophet and about what will happen to people at the Last Judgment. These suras are known as Makki because they were revealed in Makka. They are the shortest suras, and are at the end of the *Quran*. Later suras give Muslims guidance for their everyday lives and deal with matters such as marriage, law and helping other people within the Muslim community, or umma. The words in the *Quran* and the book itself are treated with the greatest respect, and making a beautiful copy of some or all of the words is an act of worship and thanksgiving.

THE *HADITH*

Muslims can find further advice and guidance in books known as the *Hadith*. These are collections of the sayings of Muhammad, together with his opinions and an account of his actions. They were all gathered together after his death and include advice such as, 'Do not sit between two men without the permission of both', and 'Wealth comes from a contented heart, not a lot of possessions'. The *Hadith* also contain instructions such as, 'All Muslim men and women must seek knowledge'. There are several different collections of *Hadith*, but the most reliable version is that of Imam Bukhari who lived in the 9th century CE.

INSIDE A MOSQUE

The Muslims' place of worship is known as a mosque, which means 'place of prostration'. The first mosque was built in Madina for Muhammad and his followers and was a simple structure, made from tree-trunks and palm leaves. Later mosques were built from brick or stone, and were often beautifully decorated with patterned tiles and fine plasterwork. Most of them have a tall tower, or

The minaret on the Qiblatan Mosque in Madina

minaret, from the top of which a man known as the muezzin calls the faithful to prayer. Inside the mosque there is an open courtyard with a fountain, called a fawwara, where worshippers can wash themselves before praying. Beyond the courtyard is the covered prayer-hall, known as the zulla. This is often domed and divided into two parts, so that men and women can pray separately. An arch in the wall, called the mihrab, indicates the direction of Makka so that worshippers know in which direction to face for their prayers. Next to the mihrab is the minbar. This is a tall pulpit from which sermons are given by the prayer-leader, or imam.

Inside the Mohammad Ali Mosque in Cairo, Egypt. The mihrab is on the left and the minbar is on the right.

CHAPTER FIVE

THE UMAYYADS AND THE ABBASIDS

The Muslims were united by their religion, rather than by nationality or politics, and the head of their community, or umma, was also their spiritual leader. This leader was always a man and was known as the caliph, a name which comes from the Arabic Khalifat-ur-Rasul Allah, meaning 'successor of the Messenger of God'.

MUHAMMAD'S SUCCESSORS

When Muhammad died in Madina in 632 CE, his close friend and father-in-law Abu Bakr was elected to take over his role as leader of the Muslim community and was the first to be given the title Khalifat-ur-Rasul Allah. Under Abu Bakr's leadership, the whole of Arabia was brought under Muslim control. When he died in 634, Islam had already begun to spread into Iraq and Syria. The second caliph was Umar I. During his ten-year reign the Muslim armies conquered Syria and Iraq and started their conquest of Egypt and Iran. Like Abu Bakr, Umar ruled from Madina, but Makka remained the religious centre of the growing empire. Umar ordered that the complete message brought by the angel to Muhammad from Allah should be written down while people could still remember exactly what had been said.

These pages are from the oldest surviving handwritten copy of the Quran. It was made in 640 CE and is decorated with real gold.

Chapter Five

When Umar was murdered by one of his servants in 644, Uthman was elected as caliph. Uthman's reign lasted until 656 when he was also murdered. Ali, Muhammad's cousin and his son-in-law through his marriage to Fatima, the daughter of Muhammad and Khadija, was then invited to become the fourth caliph. He accepted reluctantly and had to fight two rebellions against his rule. He, too, was assassinated in 661. His main opponent, Mu'awiya of the Umayyad clan of the Quraish tribe, then came to power.

The Hand of Fatima is a symbol of the Shi'a Muslims. The thumb and four fingers represent Muhammad, his daughter Fatima, her husband Ali, and their two sons Hasan and Husain.

Sunnis and Shi'as

The only long-lasting division in Islamic belief occurred after the death of Ali. It related to who should be the next caliph. The majority believed that it should be the person who was most likely to uphold all the traditions (known as sunna) of Muhammad. These people became known as the Sunni. However, some Muslims felt that the caliphs should be chosen from the direct descendants of Muhammad. As Fatima was the only one of Muhammad's children to have lived long enough to have children of her own, Muhammad's descendants were related to Ali. His supporters called themselves shi'at Ali, which means 'the party of Ali', and they became known as the Shi'a. They believed that Ali and Fatima's son,

Husain, should have been the next caliph instead of Mu'awiyah. When Husain was killed in 680, they believed that his son, Ali, should be caliph. But, in spite of these differences, both the Sunni and the Shi'a based their lives and beliefs around the Five Pillars of Islam.

THE UMAYYAD DYNASTY

The Umayyad dynasty was founded in 661, when Mu'awiya came to power, and lasted until 750 when the last Umayyad caliph was killed at the battle of the Great Zab River. In that time the capital was moved to Damascus and the Arabs took their Islamic faith as far west as Spain and as far east as Sind in India, and Bukhara, Samarkand and Tashkent in Central Asia. Arabic became the official language throughout the empire and Arabs replaced the former administrators in the newly conquered countries. New coins were designed for use all over the empire and a postal service was set up between Damascus and the most important towns in the provinces. A strong army housed in garrison cities helped the Umayyads to keep control over their expanding empire. In the early years of Umayyad rule non-Arab Muslims, Jews and Christians were more heavily taxed than Arab Muslims. The money from this taxation helped to pay for the running of the huge empire. From 743, however, revolts against the Umayyads began to grow and in 750 they were overthrown, hunted down and killed. Only one member of the Umayyad

A CLOSER LOOK

In the early days of the empire, the Islamic army was made up of volunteers, most of whom were Arab tribesmen. Many went to live in garrison cities such as Kufa and Basra, and eventually settled there with their families. Once this happened, they often did not want to go out campaigning against rebels in far-away places, so a professional army was recruited to take their places. Most of the soldiers for this army came from Syria, but they were sent to garrisons all over the empire.

Inside the Great Mosque at Cordoba, Spain. Construction began in 786 in the reign of Abd ar-Rahman. It was extended in the 9th and 10th centuries when many of these pillars and arches were added.

family, Abd ar-Rahman, managed to escape and he went to Spain where he founded the Umayyad dynasty in Cordoba.

THE ABBASID DYNASTY

After the defeat of the Umayyads, the Abbasids came to power. They took their name from Muhammad's uncle, Abbas, from whom they were descended. Under their rule, the Islamic empire began to change. Though the Islamic religion continued to expand by trade and other peaceful means, the great conquests ended. Non-Arab Muslims now outnumbered Arab Muslims, and their influence started to increase. This was especially true of the Persians, who had been the strongest supporters of the Abbasids in their rise to power. As a result, the Abbasid caliphs based their ideas of government on a combination of those of the former Sasanian Empire (see page 35) and the teachings of the Islamic religion. Makka and

The spiral minaret at the Great Mosque of al-Muttawakkil in Samarra. It was built around 850 and is still the largest mosque in the world. Today, Samarra is a centre of pilgrimage for Shi'a Muslims.

Madina continued to be the great spiritual and religious centres but, in 762, al-Mansur, the second Abbasid caliph, started to build a new administrative capital at Baghdad.

During the reign of Harun ar-Rashid (786-809), Baghdad was thought to be the richest city in the world, but less than 30 years after his death it had been partly destroyed in a civil war. The caliph and his court built a new capital at Samarra, but returned to Baghdad in 892. By that time, Abbasid power was weakening and people who were not of Arab origin were becoming even more powerful. Most important amongst them were the Fatimids, who took control of Tunisia in 909 and conquered Egypt in 969, and the Seljuqs who overpowered the Abbasids in 1055. The Abbasid caliphs continued as religious leaders until 1258, when the Mongols attacked Baghdad and the Abbasid dynasty came to an end.

LIFE AS A MUSLIM

For all Muslims, religion was the most important part of everyday life and whatever they did had to fit into the pattern of prayers, fasts and feasts that made up part of the Five Pillars of Islam. Their

A CLOSER LOOK

The Seljuqs were a Turkish dynasty, led by Toghril Beg. In 1063 he was succeeded by his nephew, Alp Arslan, who defeated the Byzantines at the battle of Manzikert in 1071, and opened up Asia Minor to the Muslim faith. He was followed by his son, Malik-Shah, who built his capital at Isfahan and was a great patron of science and the arts. Although Malik-Shah was the head of state, or sultan, the real power belonged to Nizam al-Mulk who was his chief minister, or vizier. When Malik-Shah and Nizam al-Mulk both died in 1092, Seljuq power began to decline.

A CLOSER LOOK

In the centre of Baghdad stood the caliph's palace and the grand mosque. Four roads divided the city into four equal quarters where the caliph's officials and courtiers lived. This part of the city was surrounded by three concentric walls, beyond which the merchants built their bazaars and houses. At the other side of the River Tigris was the palace of the heir apparent, surrounded by more houses and workshops. Traders brought goods from as far away as India, China and East Africa to the riverside wharves and even the Vikings visited occasionally. Scholars, artists and craftworkers were all attracted to the city, which had a university, hospitals, bath houses and an observatory, as well as many beautiful mosques.

Musicians of the caliphs of Baghdad

religion also gave them rules to live by which were based on the teachings of the *Quran* and on the thoughts of Muhammad as written down in the *Hadith*. These rules told Muslims what was forbidden, or haram, and what was allowed, or halal. Forbidden things included drinking alcohol, eating pork, any kind of gambling, charging interest on financial loans, telling lies, stealing, and committing murder or suicide. Meat could only be halal if the butcher had said the prayer, 'Allah Akbar' (meaning 'God is great') three times over the animal before killing it by cutting its throat.

CHAPTER SIX

THE SPREAD OF ISLAM

By the time of Muhammad's death, the Islamic faith was spreading quickly throughout Arabia. Under the leadership of Abu Bakr (see page 29), the whole of the region was brought under Muslim control. But Muslims were determined to extend their faith beyond the boundaries of Arabia.

THE BYZANTINE AND SASANIAN EMPIRES

During Muhammad's lifetime, the north of Arabia was sandwiched between the two mighty empires of the Byzantines and the Sasanians. The lands of the

Desert landscape near Fars in present-day Iran. In the time of Muhammad this region was part of the Sasanian Empire.

Chapter Six

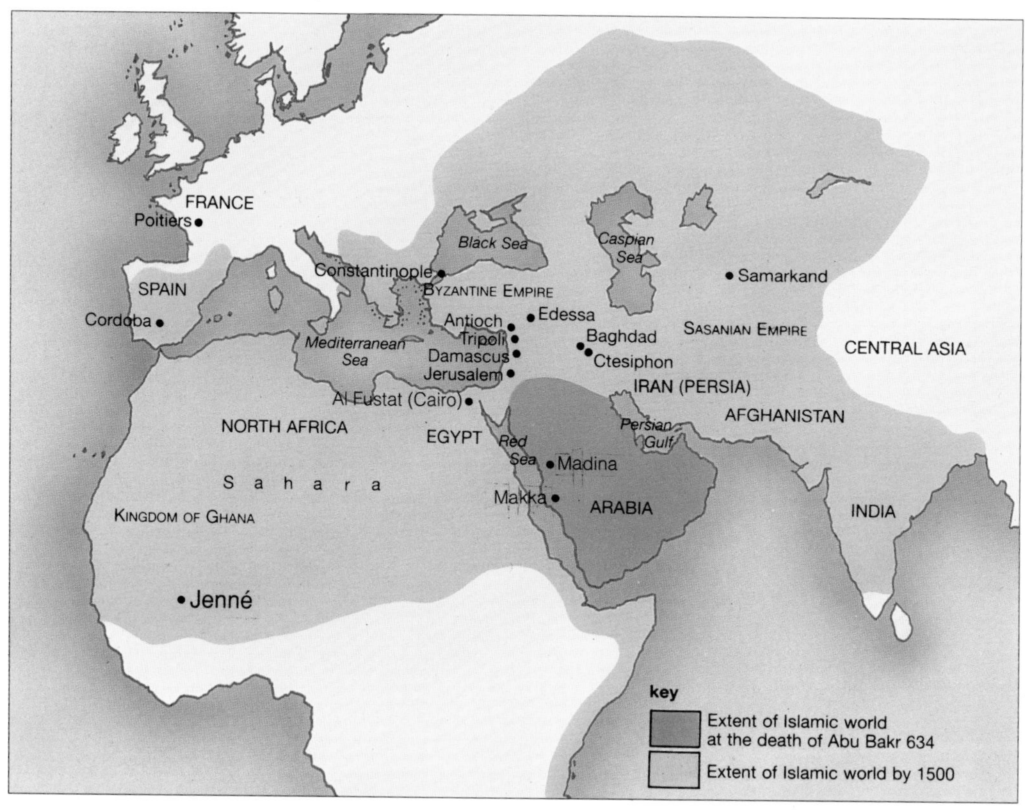

This map shows how the Muslim world expanded btween 634 and 1500.

Byzantine Empire lay to the north and west and were ruled from Constantinople. To the north and east lay the lands of the Sasanian Empire, ruled from Ctesiphon. These empires frequently went to war against each other. However, both needed to maintain a good relationship with the Arabs as, in order to trade with India and other distant lands, Byzantine ships sailed down the Red Sea and Sasanian ships down the Persian Gulf.

Neither the Byzantines nor the Sasanians had tried to conquer Arabia because most of its land and its people were too poor to add any wealth to their empires. In contrast, the Arabs often carried out raids into both Byzantine and Sasanian territory, but these were usually small-scale and soon defeated. This is what happened to Muhammad's first expedition to Byzantine Syria in 629. However, the Byzantines and Sasanians were so accustomed to defeating the Arabs, that they were both taken by surprise when larger Muslim armies began to attack in earnest.

ISLAM SPREADS NORTHWARDS

A CLOSER LOOK
Although the Muslims hoped that the people they conquered would convert to their faith, Jews and Christians were allowed to follow their own religions. However, to make up for not paying zakat (see page 23), Jews and Christians were required to pay higher taxes than Muslims.

In 634 Abu Bakr sent an army northwards towards the Sasanian Empire. Led by Khalid ibn al-Walid, it soon conquered part of what is now Iraq, then marched across the Syrian desert to attack the Byzantine city of Damascus. Once the Muslims had defeated the Byzantines in Damascus, they marched south and in 638 CE entered Jerusalem. Led by the new caliph, Umar (see page 29), the Muslims took control of the city, which was a holy place to them, as well as to the Jews and the Christians. From there they turned towards Egypt which was part of the Byzantine Empire.

ISLAM SPREADS WESTWARDS

The Muslims invaded Egypt in 639 CE with an army of around 4000 men. By 642 the Byzantine army

A CLOSER LOOK
The rock from which Muhammad made his ascent into Heaven (see page 21) was on the site of the Jewish temple in Jerusalem. After the Muslims took control of the city they built a mosque, known as the Dome of the Rock, around it. The Dome of the Rock was erected between 685 and 692 CE.

A view of the Dome of the Rock in Jerusalem

Chapter Six

The Alhambra Palace in Granada is one of the many buildings erected in Spain by the Muslims that can still be seen today. It was built between 1238 and 1358 and its name comes from an Arabic word meaning 'the red', after the colour of its walls.

had left and the Muslims were in control. They founded a new capital called Al Fustat (present-day Cairo) and then set out to conquer the rest of the North African coast. There, as in Egypt, they came across many people who were Christians or Jews. They also encountered some Berbers who fiercely resisted their invasion. But there were many more people who wanted to become Muslims and follow the Islamic way of life. By 697 they had conquered Carthage and by the year 700 the Muslim invaders controlled almost the whole length of the North African coast.

In 711 the Muslims crossed the Straits of Gibraltar and began the conquest of Spain and Portugal, which at that time were both ruled by the Visigoths. By 732 they had crossed into France and attacked Bordeaux. They got as far as the town of Poitiers before they were firmly defeated in battle by the Frankish ruler, Charles Martel. After this battle, the Muslims did not try to venture any further north, but they continued to control large parts of Spain and Portugal for several more centuries.

ISLAM CROSSES THE SAHARA

In North Africa, the Muslim armies were quickly followed by Arab merchants and traders who wanted to set up businesses in the newly conquered lands. Trade routes had long been established between the ports on the Mediterranean coast and the grasslands and rainforests to the south of the Sahara. Many of these routes passed through the Kingdom of Ghana (which was much further north than the present-day country of Ghana). During the 10th century, the Kingdom of Ghana controlled the trade in gold from the south and salt from the north. People captured in the south to be sold into slavery were also taken to Ghana, while woollen cloth and luxury items were taken there from the north. Arab traders soon became involved in this trade, using large numbers of camels to transport goods across the desert. They took their religion with them and, by 1100 CE, most of the people living along the southern edge of the Sahara had become Muslims.

The Great Mosque at Jenne in Mali was first built in the 14th century. Its mud-brick walls have been replaced many times since then, but its basic plan has stayed the same.

Chapter Six

Islam spreads to the east

While one Muslim army was conquering large parts of the Byzantine Empire, another was heading north and east, taking control of the region that is present-day Iraq by 629. The Muslims continued east and, by 705, had also conquered Iran and Afghanistan. After this they took their religion into India and the steppes of central Asia, and along the trade routes into the Chinese Empire. The spread across India was gradual and there were separate conquests of different areas at different times. From the 10th century, some of the Turkish tribes on the Asian steppes began to spread the Islamic faith westwards again into Anatolia and Turkey, which were still part of the Byzantine Empire.

This French picture from the 14th century shows Christian knights and their followers preparing to set out on a crusade against the Muslims. Many of the Crusaders were away from their homes for several years.

The clash with the Christians

By the 11th century, many of the countries of Europe were richer and more stable than they had been in the 8th century. Christianity was firmly established and trade and commerce were

A CLOSER LOOK

Salah ad-Din (Saladin) was one of the great Muslim heroes. Born around 1137, he became vizier of Egypt and commander of the Syrian army in 1169. Two years later, he became the sole ruler, or sultan, of Egypt which was a very rich country. He used Egyptian wealth to finance a campaign which added Syria, Palestine and northern Mesopotamia to his empire by 1186. He then united the Muslims into a well-organised army to fight against the Crusaders. He defeated the Crusaders at the battle of Hattin in July 1187 and went on to take control of Jerusalem in October of that year. Unlike the Crusaders, Saladin and his troops treated the people of Jerusalem fairly and with courtesy. By 1192 he had forced the knights of the third crusade to return to Europe, but, exhausted by his long and arduous campaigns, he died in March 1193.

expanding. Many people started going on pilgrimages to Jerusalem and other places in the East associated with Christianity. The Muslims allowed Christians access across their territory, but in 1095 Pope Urban II decided that this was not enough. He called for a Christian army to set out and capture Jerusalem from the Muslims.

This Christian army was made up of knights from various countries. In 1099 the army reached Jerusalem, taking control of the city and killing all the Muslims and Jews they found there. Over the next few years the Christian knights, who called themselves Crusaders, also took control of the Muslim cities of Edessa, Antioch and Tripoli. When the Muslims recaptured Edessa in 1144, a second crusade was sent out. A third crusade was launched in 1189 following the recapture of Jerusalem by the Muslims under the leadership of Salah ad-Din (Saladin). But the Crusaders could not repeat their earlier successes. By 1291 they had lost all the territory gained in the first crusade. However, those who returned to Europe took back scientific knowledge and other ideas that were far in advance of scholarship in their own countries. They also returned with foods such as cane sugar, citrus fruits and spices which had rarely been seen before in Western Europe.

Genghis Khan became ruler of the Mongols in 1206. Before turning their attention to the Muslim world, the Mongols had already captured Beijing and large parts of northern China.

THE MONGOLS ATTACK

During the 13th century, the Mongols (from the steppes of eastern Asia) brought terror and destruction to many parts of the Islamic world. Led by their ruler, Genghis Khan, the Mongols overran Persia, Turkestan and Afghanistan between 1218 and 1225. Genghis Khan's son conquered Armenia and Tibet and attacked Hungary and Poland. Then in the 1250s, his grandson, Hulagu, set out to conquer the regions that are present-day Iran and Iraq, making them part of the Mongol Empire. In 1258 Hulagu destroyed Baghdad and executed the last caliph. However, when he tried to conquer Syria and Egypt in 1260, he was defeated by the Mamluks, a dynasty of slave-soldiers who had recently taken power in Egypt.

For about 100 years after the destruction of Baghdad, the Mongols took control of huge areas in the east of what had been the Abbasid and Seljuq empires. They began to rebuild the cities they had destroyed and encouraged learning and the arts throughout their empire. They appointed Persian-speaking administrators to help them run their part of the former Abbasid Empire and, in 1295, the Mongol leader became a Muslim.

A CLOSER LOOK

The Muslim Ibn al-Athir wrote that the Mongols 'in just one year seized... the most beautiful and the best cultivated part of the earth... In the countries which have not yet been overrun by them, everyone spends the night afraid that they may appear there too.' Genghis Khan is said to have wanted to destroy all the towns and cities he came across and let the land that they were built on return to steppe, where his people could graze their flocks of sheep, cattle and horses.

Part of the Registan Square in Tamerlane's capital, Samarkand. Three sides of the square are made up of madrassas (Islamic colleges), each of which is beautifully decorated with blue and turquoise tiles.

When the huge Mongol Empire broke up in 1294, many of its lesser chiefs gained small states and empires of their own. One of these states was Turkestan with its capital at Samarkand. In 1370, Tamerlane became its ruler. He was a ferocious warrior and by 1401 he had conquered Persia, occupied Moscow, invaded India and defeated Syria. He was also a Muslim, and a great patron of the arts. He employed craftsmen from many parts of the Islamic world to work in Samarkand. After his death, his empire was divided among his four sons, all of whom were more interested in studying Islam than in conquering more lands.

TOWARDS NEW EMPIRES

By the 14th century, the Islamic world was changing. Although its people were still united by their religion, its area was so vast that it was impossible for one person to control it all. New dynasties came to power in different areas. Some controlled only small amounts of land and lasted for no more than two or three generations, but others began to build up large empires. The most important of these dynasties were the Safavids in Persia, the Mughals in India and the Ottomans in Turkey. You can find out more about them in Chapter Nine.

CHAPTER SEVEN

SCIENCE AND TECHNOLOGY

Muslims believed that Allah had created everything in the world and beyond it. Because of this, they thought that studying and learning more about the world would help them to a better understanding of Allah. Muhammad himself encouraged his followers to leave home if necessary in search of knowledge, saying they would be walking in the way of Allah if they did so.

The dome of the Mir-i-Arab Madrassa in Bukhara in present-day Uzbekistan. It dates from the 17th century. As well as studying Islamic religion and law, scholars in the madrassa studied Arabic literature, mathematics and science.

PRESERVING ANCIENT KNOWLEDGE

Over 1000 years before the birth of Muhammad, Greece was the centre of science and learning for people who lived around the Mediterranean Sea. Scholars studied philosophy and mathematics, astronomy, medicine, geography and history and wrote down their findings for others to read. However, from the 4th century CE onwards, some of these studies clashed with the teachings of the Christian church. Certain scholars were labelled heretics and forced to flee to escape persecution. Some went to Persia where they met other scholars from India and China, two countries where knowledge was also thought to be important. They shared and developed their ideas, helping to keep the ancient knowledge alive and adding to it as new discoveries were made. Later both the Umayyad and the Abbasid caliphs invited scholars from all parts of their empires, including Persia, to visit their courts in Damascus and Baghdad.

A CLOSER LOOK
The works of the ancient Greeks were translated into Syriac and then into Arabic. Many copies were made and sent to all parts of the Islamic world. As Arabic was the language of the *Quran*, all scholars could understand it. Some of the copies that went to Spain ended up in Christian monasteries, which were tolerated by the Muslim rulers. The monks translated the Arabic into Latin, which was the language of the Christian church. Copies of these Latin translations were eventually taken to other Christian countries such as France, Germany and Britain.

MATHEMATICS, ASTRONOMY AND NAVIGATION

Mathematical knowledge was greatly valued by the Muslims. From the works of Greeks such as Euclid they gained an understanding of geometry which helped them in surveying and building mosques, palaces, forts and bridges. From India they learned about a system of numbering that was much simpler than Roman numerals. The numbers we use today are called Arabic numerals, because we, in turn, inherited them from the Arabs.

These scholars are learning how to use an astrolabe and quadrants in the 16th-century observatory of Taqi al-Din in Istanbul.

Mathematics also helped the Muslims in their study of astronomy. For their calendar, Muslims needed to calculate when each new moon was going to appear, while for the month of Ramadan they needed to know the times of sunrise and sunset each day. To make these calculations they developed scientific instruments such as the astrolabe, which was used to work out the movements of the stars and planets, and the quadrant, which measured the angle between the Earth and a star. For their prayers, Muslims also needed to know the direction of Makka. For this they used a magnetic compass, which was developed from an ancient Chinese idea.

CHAPTER SEVEN

These scientific instruments helped Muslim travellers to find their way around the world. Some of these journeys were undertaken by pilgrims making their way to Makka to take part in the yearly Hajj, while others were undertaken by traders carrying goods from as far away as China, by camel train and by ship.

This brass astrolabe was made in Cairo, Egypt, in 1236. It was used to work out the position of the sun or the stars in relation to the horizon.

GEOGRAPHY

Muslim geographers knew that the world was round like a ball, rather than like a disc, and their mathematicians were able to calculate both its circumference and its diameter. One geographer, Al-Idrisi, was born in north Africa around 1100 CE. He produced accurate maps of the world as it was known then. Other Muslim travellers wrote books about what they saw and the people they met on their journeys. In 10th-century Egypt, Al-Masudi wrote a 30-volume encyclopaedia describing the countries he had visited, while Al-Biruni, who died in 1050, wrote a geography of India. One of the most famous Arab travellers was Ibn Battuta. He was born in Tangier in 1304 and had travelled over 100,000 kilometres in Muslim lands by the time he died in 1377.

A CLOSER LOOK

The word monsoon comes from the Arabic word *mausim*, which was used to describe the seasonal winds in the Arabian Sea. These winds blow from the northeast for one half of the year and from the southwest for the other half. Arab sailors learned how to use the monsoon winds to speed up their journeys to and from India.

Some Arab travellers ventured north into the lands of the Vikings. In 922 Ibn Fadlan, an Arab ambassador, wrote a detailed description of the funeral of a Viking chief which he witnessed on the banks of the River Volga. Another Arab traveller, Al-Tattushi, visited the Viking market town of Hedeby in Denmark and wrote that the men as well as the women wore make-up on their eyes. He also added that when they sang it sounded like dogs howling, but worse!

A pharmacist prepares a remedy for an illness in this illustration from a 13th-century copy of the Materia Medica *by Dioscorides.*

MEDICINE

Another area in which the Muslims excelled was medicine. Their scholars translated books from the Greek, the most important of which were the works of the ancient Greek physician Galen who lived in the 2nd century CE, and of the pharmacologist Dioscorides who lived in the 1st century CE. To this information the Muslims added medical knowledge from India and from their own studies. They knew that diet and climate could affect people's health, and tried to treat all illnesses with herbs and drugs, rather than by surgery. By the 9th century CE there were hospitals in large cities such as Baghdad where well-trained doctors could pass on their skills to younger men. Many went on to write medical textbooks of their own. One of the most famous was *al-Qanun*, written by Ibn Sina who was born near Bukhara in central Asia in 980 CE. In it he described the symptoms of many serious diseases and how they spread, and gave a list of 760 different drugs that were currently in use.

Pictures like this helped Muslim doctors and pharmacists to recognise the plants they needed to make up their remedies.

KNOWLEDGE FROM CHINA

As well as importing silk, porcelain and spices from China, Muslim traders also brought back practical knowledge based on Chinese inventions. One of these inventions was paper-making. Another was wood-block printing. This made it possible to produce copies of a book far more quickly than by writing them out by hand, and so allowed knowledge to spread more widely. Gunpowder also came from China and, by the early 14th century CE, the Muslims had discovered how to make it and use it to fire arrows from a very simple gun. This knowledge also spread to Europe, changing the face of warfare for ever.

By the time the Ottoman emperor, Sulaiman I, attacked Hungary in 1543 (see pages 54-5), gunpowder was in regular use in guns and cannon.

CHAPTER EIGHT

ARTS AND CRAFTS

During the centuries after Muhammad's death, Muslim artists and craftworkers became experts at making both beautiful and practical items. Muslim architects designed mosques, palaces, tombs and gardens, and writers created stories and poems, some of which are still read today. As in all other aspects of Islamic life, the *Quran* and its teachings played an important role, and producing a fine copy of the *Quran* or any of its suras was thought of as an act of worship, as well as a work of art.

A late 13th-century plate, made in Persia.

POTTERY

Although Arab traders brought fine pottery and porcelain back from China, there were many potters in the Islamic world who made everyday items such as jars, bowls, plates and lamps. Potters often decorated these objects with geometric patterns such as circles, stars and diamonds, or with arabesques based on the intertwining pattern of leaves and stalks, usually of the acanthus plant. We know that many of these pots were traded throughout the Islamic world, because remains have been found in places as far apart as East Africa and Malaysia.

A CLOSER LOOK

In the Islamic world, human figures and pictures of animals are not permitted for decoration, especially on objects which might be used in a religious context, such as lamps or tiles for mosques. This is because it is thought that these pictures might encourage the worship of idols again, as in the past.

On the inside of an arch, tiles were often arranged in a honeycomb pattern, like these in the Friday Mosque at Shiraz, Iran.

TILE-MAKING

Many buildings, particularly mosques, palaces and the homes of the rich, were decorated with patterned and glazed pottery tiles. These tiles were often in rich, deep colours, turquoise and blue being favourites. They were decorated with geometric shapes or arabesques, or with words from the *Quran* or the *Hadith*. Sometimes the same pattern would be used over and over again on many different tiles, but sometimes several different tiles would be placed together to make up a larger pattern.

CALLIGRAPHY

The art of beautiful handwriting, known as calligraphy, was highly valued in the world of Islam. Calligraphy was written on parchment and paper, and on pottery and tiles. The words were formed with pens made from sharpened reeds, dipped into ink. Usually the words were written as

The curves and scrolls on this example of calligraphy are known as arabesques. Their shapes are based on the stalks and leaves of plants.

straightforward pieces of text, but sometimes the letters were arranged so that they formed geometric shapes or pictures. Pictures of boats and birds were especially popular. They were made either from the letters of the Arabic alphabet or from prayers, blessings and religious phrases. As well as being decorative, this writing reminded people of the words of Allah as they were dictated to Muhammad.

TEXTILES

Long before the birth of Muhammad, the nomadic people of Arabia made textiles for practical purposes. They spun and wove hair and wool from their sheep, goats and camels to make the tents in which they lived, and the clothes they wore. In a land where wood was scarce, they also wove cloth to make cushions to sit on, instead of chairs, and bags in which to store their belongings, instead of chests or cupboards. These cushions and bags were also easy to carry around when the nomads were on the move. Most of these early items were plain or had a simple striped pattern, but later carpets and rugs were often richly decorated. These carpets were traded over long distances.

A CLOSER LOOK

Women from rich families often wore heavy necklaces, bracelets and rings made from gold and set with semi-precious stones and jewels. This jewellery was worn not only as a personal decoration, but also to show the wealth and importance of their families.

Chapter Eight

Architecture

The Muslims excelled at architecture. They were helped by their interest in mathematics which they used to make the calculations needed to plan elaborate domes, arches, pillars and minarets. These were features of mosques and other important buildings. As well as being covered with coloured tiles, many of these buildings were also decorated with fine plasterwork and exquisite stone carvings,

The exquisite stonework in the Court of Lions at the Alhambra Palace in Granada, Spain.

Pools and fountains were popular features in gardens in the Islamic world. They helped to create a cool atmosphere where people could sit or walk in comfort.

A CLOSER LOOK

After the 8th century, a lot of poetry was written by people known as Sufis. These were both men and women who tried to get as close to God as possible in their everyday lives. Their name came from the rough woollen cloak, or *suf*, which they often wore to show that they were not interested in comfort or possessions. Some of the ways in which they tried to get close to God included going without food or sleep, chanting, studying deeply and meditating.

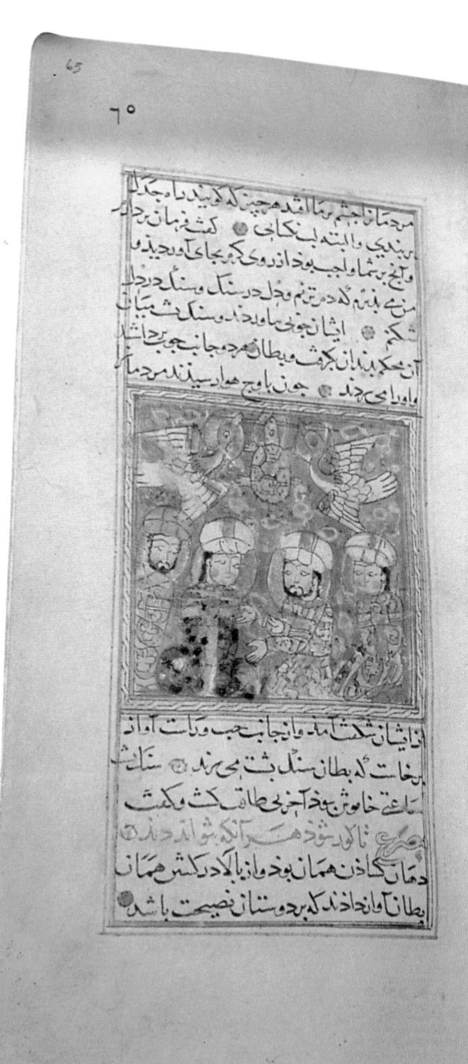

This colourful illustration is from the legend of Humay and Humayan in a 14th-century manuscript from Baghdad.

usually in geometric designs. Palaces and large houses were decorated in a similar way, and were often built around open courtyards with at least one garden. There were separate quarters where the women lived in privacy and brought up their children away from the bustle of court or business concerns.

POETS AND STORYTELLERS

Poetry and storytelling were both very popular throughout the Muslim world, as they had been in Arabia in the time before Muhammad was born. The best known collection of stories from the Muslim world was written for entertainment. *The Thousand and One Arabian Nights* contains stories from China, Egypt and India, as well as from Arabia. These stories were collected over many years, but probably starting in the reign of Harun ar-Rashid (see page 33). Some of the famous stories in this collection are 'Aladdin', 'Ali Baba and the Forty Thieves' and 'Sinbad the Sailor'. Many of the books of poems and stories were illustrated with detailed, coloured pictures, showing various aspects of Muslim life, especially from the Mughal and Ottoman empires (see Chapter Nine).

CHAPTER NINE

THE LATER EMPIRES

Both the Umayyads and the Abbasids used provincial governors to help them rule their vast empires. Sometimes these governors became powerful enough to set up dynasties of their own, such as that of the Fatimids in Egypt, but throughout this period the caliph in Damascus and later in Baghdad continued to be leader of the Islamic world. After the attacks by the Mongols in the 13th century, this situation changed. Baghdad and many of its neighbouring towns and cities were destroyed and their inhabitants either fled or were killed. Only the Mamluks (see page 42) were able to prevent the Mongols from spreading into the western part of the Muslim world. By the 1330s, however, the Mongols' power was waning and the first of the new Islamic empires was starting its rise to power.

A CLOSER LOOK

The last Abbasid caliph was killed when the Mongols destroyed his capital at Baghdad, but some members of his family managed to escape and made their way to Cairo, the Mamluk capital in Egypt. They were given sanctuary and the caliph continued to be chosen from their descendants until 1517, when the Mamluks were finally overthrown by the Ottomans.

THE OTTOMAN EMPIRE

The first of the new empires to emerge was that of the Ottomans. It had its origins in the early 14th century when Osman, a Turkish chief, began to attack and conquer parts of the Byzantine Empire. By 1453 one of his descendants, Mehmet II, was powerful enough to capture the Byzantine capital, Constantinople, and turn it into the capital for his own empire, with the new name of Istanbul. By 1500 this empire included Greece, Turkey and the Crimea. Expansion continued in the reign of Selim II (1512-20).

Under Selim's son, Sulaiman I (1520-66), the Ottoman Empire entered a Golden Age. Istanbul

The Sulaimaniye Mosque in Istanbul was built between 1550 and 1557. The complex also contained four madrassas, a medical school and hospital, and the tombs of Sulaiman I and his wife, Haseki Hurrem.

stood at the crossroads of trade routes between Asia and Europe and its markets generated wealth by selling goods from as far away as China and England. This wealth helped Sulaiman to expand his empire to include Budapest, most of Hungary, Croatia, Armenia and parts of what is now Iraq. He even made an attack on Vienna, the capital of the Holy Roman Empire. Under Sulaiman, arts and crafts, literature, carpet-weaving, architecture and education also flourished.

A portrait of the Ottoman emperor, Sulaiman I

A CLOSER LOOK
Many people in the Ottoman Empire were Orthodox Christians. They were allowed to keep their religion so long as they paid a tribute to the Ottoman rulers. This tribute could be in money or in service, and many Orthodox Christians fought alongside Muslims in battles against the Holy Roman Empire. Others converted to Islam and became civil servants, government officers or Janissaries, soldiers whose job was to protect the sultan.

Sulaiman's son, Selim II, did not share his father's enthusiasm for government. He preferred to lead a life of leisure while his ministers and generals did all the work of running the empire on his behalf. They encouraged him to invade Cyprus in 1570. This brought the Ottomans into direct conflict with the Holy Roman Empire, Spain, and the state of Venice which had control of Cyprus. These countries sent a combined fleet to attack Selim's navy at Lepanto in the Gulf of Corinth in October 1571. In the years that followed, the countries of Europe and Asia began to trade directly with each other instead of sending their goods through the markets of Istanbul. This took some of the Ottomans' wealth, but their empire was set to last until the 20th century.

A CLOSER LOOK
While new Muslim empires were gathering strength in the east, the Muslims were slowly losing control of Spain. This was because the Christian rulers in Spain were becoming more powerful. In 1492, the armies of Ferdinand of Aragon and his wife Isabella of Castile defeated the last of the Muslims in Granada and united Spain into one, Christian, country.

THE SAFAVID EMPIRE

The second empire to emerge was that of the Safavids. It was founded in 1501 when Ismail I captured the city of Tabriz in what is now Iran and declared himself ruler, or shah, of Azerbaijan. By 1502, he was powerful enough to be declared shah of Iran and in the next ten years he took control of most of Iran and parts of what are present-day Iraq.

Ismail named his empire after his ancestor, Safi-ud-Din (1253-1334), who had been head of the Sufi order of Safawiyya and followed the Sunni branch of Islam. However, in around 1399, descendants of Safi-ud-Din decided to become members of the Shi'a party. In Ismail's reign, this led to conflict between the Shi'a Safavids and the neighbouring Ottoman Empire which followed the Sunni branch. The

The dome of the Lotfollah mosque as seen from the Royal Mosque in Isfahan. Both were started in the reign of Abbas I (1588-1629), but the Royal Mosque was not completed until after his death.

Safavid and Ottoman empires went to war several times in the 16th century.

These conflicts helped to weaken the Safavid Empire during the reign of Ismail's eldest son but in 1588 a new shah, Abbas I, renewed its fortunes. He trained an army which was capable of defeating the Ottomans, and recaptured the land they had lost in earlier wars. He also set up a new system of administration. Industry and communications within his empire were improved and trade with the West was expanded to bring in more wealth. He made his capital at Isfahan and turned it into a city of great architectural beauty. After the death of Abbas I in 1629, the Safavid Empire began to decline once more, finally falling in 1732.

Babur, founder of the Mughal dynasty, was a military genius. He was also a gifted poet and a lover of nature who enjoyed creating gardens wherever he went. This 17th-century picture shows him sitting in one of these gardens while dictating to one of his secretaries.

THE MUGHAL EMPIRE

The third empire was that of the Mughals. The Mughals were descended from Tamerlane (see page 43) and from the Mongol leader, Genghis Khan. This empire was founded by Babur who became ruler of Ferghana in Turkestan at the end of the 15th century. From there he took control of Kabul in Afghanistan and used it as a base for raids on northern India. In 1526 Babur's army went as far as the plains of India, where it defeated the forces of the Sultan of Delhi. After conquering the Rajputs near Agra in the following year, Babur took control of the whole of northern India, becoming the first of the Mughal rulers.

After Babur's death in 1530, his son, Humayun, almost lost his father's empire. After ten years of fighting, he was forced out of India. By 1555, he had started to reconquer his empire, but in 1556 he was killed in an accident.

When Humayun's son, Akbar, inherited the Mughal throne, he found himself ruling over a country divided by many warring factions, as Hindus and Muslims fought for control. Akbar tried to solve the problem by treating people of both religions equally and by marrying a Hindu princess. He also built a new capital for his empire at Fatehpur Sikri in Uttar Pradesh, using a mixture of Muslim and Hindu styles of architecture. Unfortunately the site did not have enough water to support a large population and it was used from only 1569 to 1585, when the capital moved back to Agra. Under Akbar, who died in 1605, and his son Jahangir, who ruled from 1605 to 1627, the Mughal Empire expanded and

Work started on the Taj Mahal in 1632 and took about 22 years to complete. The mausoleum, shown here, is made of white marble, carved with verses from the Quran. *It contains the tombs of both Mumtaz Mahal and Shah Jahan.*

flourished. Literature, painting and architecture were all encouraged, as were trade and industry, while the amount of land under Mughal control was increased. However, it was Jahangir's son, Shah Jahan (ruled 1628-58) who built the most famous monument of the Mughal Empire, when he erected the Taj Mahal at Agra in memory of his wife, Mumtaz Mahal.

TIMELINE

c. 570 Muhammad is born in Makka.
610 Muhammad receives the first of his messages from Allah in the cave at Hira.
613 Muhammad starts to preach in Makka.
622 Muhammad leaves Makka and goes to preach in Yathrib (later known as Madina). This event is known as the Hijra and marks the start of the Muslims' calendar.
624 Battle of Badr
625 The Battle of Uhud between the Muslims and the Makkans ends in stalemate.
628 Muhammad returns to Makka.
630 Muhammad visits Makka again and converts the Makkans to Islam.
632 Muhammad dies in Madina. Abu Bakr becomes caliph.
634 Death of Abu Bakr. Umar I becomes caliph.
638 Muslim army captures Jerusalem from the Byzantines.
639 Muslim army invades Egypt.
642 Muslims take control of Egypt and set out to conquer the North African coast.
644 Umar I is assassinated and Uthman becomes the third caliph.
656 Uthman is assassinated and Ali becomes the fourth caliph.
661 Ali is assassinated and the Umayyads come to power.
680 Ali's son Husain is killed at the Battle of Karbala.
711 Muslim conquest of Spain and Portugal starts.
732 Muslim army crosses into France and is defeated by Charles Martel at Poitiers.
750 The Umayyads are overthrown and the Abbasids come to power.
969 The Fatimids conquer Egypt.
1055 The Seljuqs take power from the Abbasids.
1071 The Seljuq ruler Alp Arslan defeats the Byzantines at Manzikert, allowing Islam to spread into Asia Minor (Turkey).
1095 Pope Urban II calls for a Christian army to capture Jerusalem from the Muslims.
1099 The knights of the first crusade capture Jerusalem from the Muslims.
1171 Saladin becomes sole ruler of Egypt.
1187 Saladin defeats the Crusaders at the battle of Hattin, before recapturing Jerusalem.
1189 A new crusade is launched, but ends in failure in 1192.
1218 The Mongols start their conquest of Persia, Turkestan and Afghanistan.
1250 The Mamluks come to power in Egypt.
1258 The Mongols overthrow the Abbasid dynasty.
1324 Death of Osman I, founder of the Ottoman Empire.
1370 Tamerlane becomes ruler of Samarkand.
1453 The Ottomans take control of the Byzantine capital, Constantinople.
1492 Christian rulers from the north of Spain take the country from the Muslims.
1501 Ismail I founds the Safavid Empire.
1517 The Ottomans defeat the Mamluks and take the title of caliph.
1519 Babur, founder of the Mughal dynasty, makes his first raid on India.
1520 The Ottoman Empire enters a Golden Age when Sulaiman I comes to power.
1526 Babur's army defeats the Sultan of Delhi's army.
1530 Death of Babur. He is succeeded by his son, Humayan.
1556 Babur's grandson, Akbar, becomes the new Mughal ruler.
1588 Abbas I becomes ruler of the Safavid Empire.
1605 Death of Akbar
1629 Death of Abbas I

GLOSSARY

arabesque – a scroll-like decoration, based on the pattern of intertwining leaves.
Bedouin – the Arabs who lead a nomadic life in desert regions.
Berber – the people who lived along the coast of North Africa.
caliph – the leader of the Islamic community.
caravanserai – an enclosed area on the trade routes across the desert where traders and their camels trains could find rest and refreshment.
dynasty – a succession of rulers from the same family.
Fatimids – a dynasty in North Africa that took its name from Muhammad's daughter, Fatima.
filigree – ornamental lacework made from carved stone, wood, pottery or metal.
garrison – a fortified place, occupied by soldiers.
Hajj – the pilgrimage to Makka in the 12th month of the Islamic year.
Hijra – Muhammad's journey from Makka to Yathrib (Madina) in 622 CE.
Holy Roman Empire – a part of Europe which included Austria, Germany and Hungary and was ruled by the Habsburg family.
imam – a leader of prayers in a mosque. Imams are often also teachers.
Janissaries – soldiers in the Ottoman Empire whose job was to protect the sultan.
jihad – a holy war undertaken by Muslims.
Mamluks – the rulers of Egypt from about 1250 to 1517.
mihrab – a niche or alcove in a mosque, showing the direction of Makka.
minaret – the tall tower on a mosque from which Muslims are called to prayer.
minbar – the tall pulpit in a mosque from which the imam delivers sermons.
Mongol – a member of one of the nomadic tribes of eastern Asia.
muezzin – the person who calls the Muslims to prayer from the minaret.
pharmacologist – someone who studies the effects of drugs on a body.
Saum – the fast from sunrise to sunset during the month of Ramadan.
Seljuqs – a Turkish dynasty that took over Abbasid power in 1055.
shah – the Persian name for a ruler or monarch.
steppes – the vast, uncultivated areas of southeast Europe and Asia.
sultan – the title given to a Muslim ruler, particularly in the Ottoman Empire.
umma – the whole Islamic community.
Visigoths – people of Germanic origin who invaded France and Spain as the Roman Empire was declining.
vizier – the most important government official in the sultan's court.
wudu – ritual washing before prayers.
zakat – an annual tax paid by Muslims to help those in need.

INDEX